Schottland
2009

mit dem Lehmbruck museum-
- Freundeskreis

M
rEmedy
S
O
S
T
I
C

```
    M
rEmedy
    S
    O
    S
    T
    I
    C
```

a compendium of mesostic poems
on the names of the 38 Bach flower remedies
composed by Alec Finlay

with contributions by Linda France

illustrated by Laurie Clark

Jupiter Artland
morning star
Ingleby Gallery
2008

naMes
makE
stemS
  chOsen
wordS
  Their
growIng
branChes

The 38 original remedies defined by Dr. Edward Bach (1886–1936) are a pharmacopeia of nature cure. Dr. Bach's philosophy of homeopathy highlighted the relationship between emotions or mental states and physical illnesses. I have composed a pair of mesostics for each remedy, to reflect the negative and positive characteristics he ascribed to them. The mesostic poem is an interleaved form, whose structure is suggestive of organic growth.

Alec Finlay

agrimony

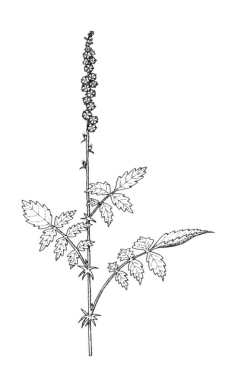

Another
meetinG
anotheR
smIle
Masking
anOther
hiddeN
anxietY

A
praGmatic
wRy
grIn
disarMs
frOwns
aNd
worrY

aspen

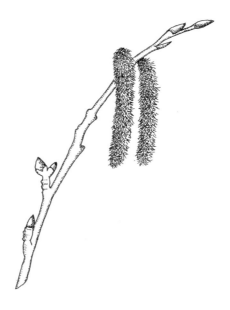

A
Sudden
Panic
strikEs
withiN

As
fearS
disapPear
lifE
sweeteNs

beech

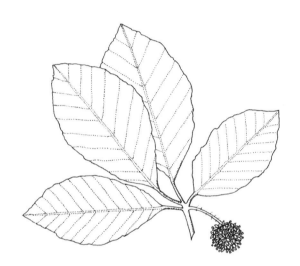

Becoming
wholE
wE
aCcept
otHers

Being
accEpted
wE
beCome
wHole

centaury

patienCe
wEars
thiN
evenTually
And
yoU
foRget
Yourself

doCile
friEnds
   Need
   Their
spAce
'yoUr'
   Respecting
'mY'

cerato

Conviction
comEs
fRom
An
inTuition
prOven

reCognise
whEn
woRds
   Are
jusT
   Opinions

cherry plum

suiCidal
   tHoughts
arE
oveRwhelming
youR
  psYche

  dePression's
overwheLming
yoUr
   Mind

suCh
overwHelming
tErrors
Require
youR
remedY

disPersing
Like
moUntain
Mist

chestnut bud

watCh
How
thE
diStant
pasT
goverNs
yoUr
presenT

Binding
yoU
rigiD

eaCh
Hurt
rEpeated
fixeS
patTerns
wouNding
yoU
furTher

unBind
yoUr
minD

chicory

eaCh
　Hurt
　Is
　aCcounted
　fOr
eveRy
　daY

Care
wHich
gIves
Caring
fOr
otheRs
selflesslY

clematis

Come
sLeep
thEn
dreaMs
hAzing
realiTy
In
cloudS

Cut
Loose
thE
soMbre
curtAins
That
blInd
uS

crab apple

superfiCial
   bRuises
     Are
      Blameless

     An
      imPerfection
  accePted
     Loses
 shamE

Clean
mirRors
Are
Beautiful

A
sPick-and-
sPan
Life's
impossiblE

elm

rEsponsibility
feeLs
overwhelMing

livE
Life
calMly

gentian

Gloomy
dEpression
turNs
lighT
Into
dArkest
Night

Give
mE
aNy
Task
I
cAn
uNdertake

gorse

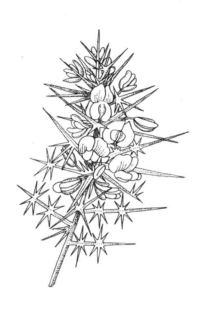

feelinG
 hOw
  eveRything
   Seems
  hopEless

Glinting
yOur
spaRkling
Self
aflamE

heather

tHeir
Ears
heAr
whaTever
tHeir
nEeds
Require

wHat
wE
shAre
  Together
 cHanges
thE
 tRuth

holly

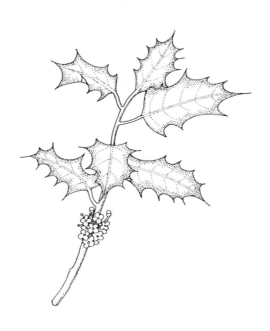

Hatred
Of
Love
fueLs
envY

tHey
fOund
Love's
peacefuL
mercY

honeysuckle

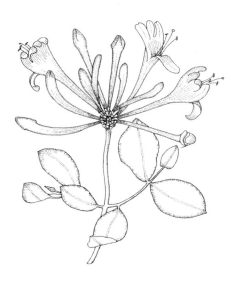

tHe
strOngest
experieNces
bEcome
memorY
kisSes
oUr
Consciousness
maKes
Last
forEver

tHe
mOst
inteNse
momEnts
staY
inSide
yoU
beComing
stucK
Like
skElfs

hornbeam

wHen
wOrk's
stRessful
theN
laBour
losEs
All
Meaning

wHen
wOrk's
caRefree
theN
laBour
dElights
plAyful
Minds

impatiens

tweakIng
    My
     Plans
    And
     Twitching
    fIngers
     nErvously
  arouNd
thumbS

thIs
seeMingly
imPossible
tAsk
isn'T
If
wE
doN't
ruSh

larch

faiLure
    Accrues
  oR
beComes
    Habitual

Life's
A
Risk
Come-on
tHen

mimulus

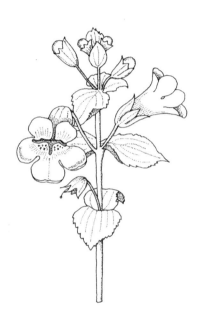

Me
knowIng
My
    Understanding
wilL
  cUre
thiS

Me
trustIng
    Myself
yoU
    Learning
yoU're
    Safe

mustard

Melancholy
withoUt
cauSe
wiThout
pAuse
oR
remeDy

soMe
tranqUil
dayS
wiTh
A
Restful
frienD

oak

despOndent
And
forsaKen

lOve
Anchors
Knowledge

olive

One
Life
Is
giVen
suffEring

One
Life
Is
giVen
pEace

pine

self-reProach
Is
stickiNg
nEedles

haPpy
In
kNowing
Enough

red chestnut

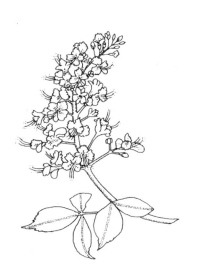

ouR
friEnds'
neeDs

eCho
tHe
vEry
needS
That
demaNd
oUr
aTtention

heR
 frEtting
  Diminishes

 Calmly
 Her
concErn
echoeS
 The
momeNt's
 aUthentic
 Truth

rock rose

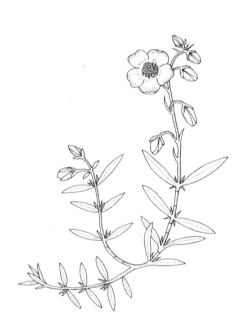

teRror
Or
shoCk
shaKes

thRough
Our
deepeSt
psychE

couRage
 grOws
   Courage
striKes

wheRever
  One
 perSon
   Endures

rock water

      Rivulets
   strOke
     Cold
rocKs

     Water
   weArs
       Through
stonE's
    stRength

Rickles
Of
Cast
rocK

floW
pAst
genTle
clEar
wateRs

scleranthus

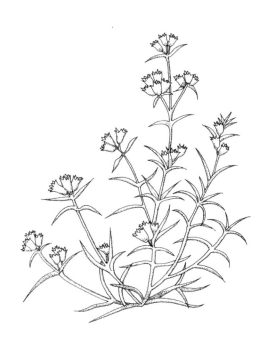

imposSible
    Choices
    Lead
   mE
nowheRe
   As
    coNstantly
   shifTing
     tHoughts
      Undermine
   deciSions

pauSe
 Consider
caLmly
 lEtting
youR
cleAr
miNd
 exTernalise
tHe
trUe
choiceS

star of bethlehem

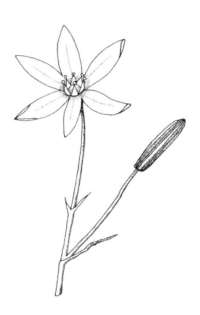

yearS
    That
    pAss
fuRl
    Our
    Feelings
    But
deEp
wiThin
  sHock's
stiLl
concEaled
wHere
no-onE
  gliMpses

dayS
    The
heArt
unfuRls

disclOsing
    Feelings

  Buried
deEp
  Trapped
witHin
muscLes
  hEaled
witH
  rEscue
reMedy

sweet chestnut

Secrets
We
concEal
bEcome
sTuck

seCrets
tHat
arE
Shared
wiTh
someoNe
trUstworthy
unsTick

everyone'S
        Worst
      fEars
        Exceed
deaTh

        Come
       sHare
        Each
         Secret
         Terror
     aNd
    trUst
one-anoTher

vervain

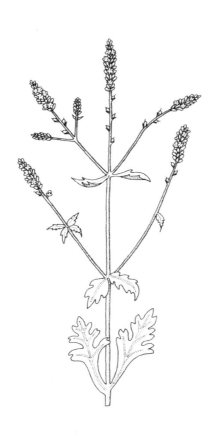

eVery
  Emotional
  Response
  Varies
  As
feelIngs
chaNge

eVery
mEntal
pRocess
reVeals
An
attItude
withiN

vine

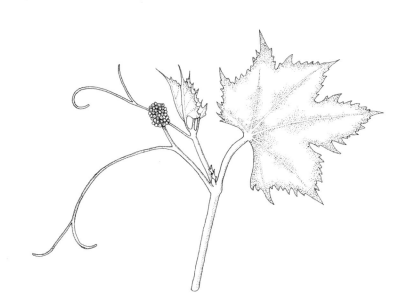

eVerything
certaIn
caN
changE

eVeryone
Is
giveN
timE

walnut

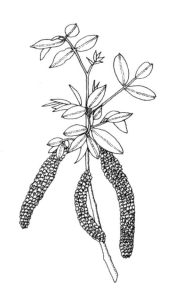

When
chAnging
bLossom
wheN
Unchanged
harvesT

We
Alone
wiLl
fiNally
cUt
knoTs

water violet

We
Are
waTer
wE
aRe

foreVer
flowIng
Or
fLoating
wE're
weT

draWn
towArds
Their
lonEly
natuRe

giVe
thIs
lOnely
souL
thEir
gifT

white chestnut

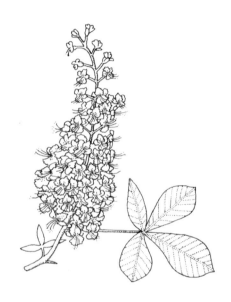

unWanted
tHoughts
persIst
wiThout
rEsolution

eaCh
nigHt
thE
wordS
That
weNt
Unsaid
repeaT

Whenever
tHose
nIght
Thoughts
rEturn

reCeive
tHe
fEar
Sense
The
healiNg
Undertone
wiThin

wild oat

Whose
lIfe
Loses
Direction

whOse
gAins
limiT?

noW
I
finaLly
realiseD

Only
todAy
maTters

wild rose

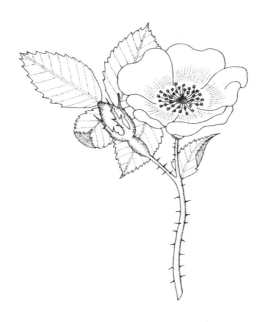

knoWing
　　wIldflowers
　wiLl
　faDe

whateveR
　grOws
　alSo
　diEs

We're
thIs
aLive
wilDness

oR
sOmething
fadeS
insidE

willow

What's
hIdden
beLow
　Leaves
nOw
shoWs

Who
Is
bLameless
bLaming
Others
Who?

notes

notes

Mesostic Remedy

Artist concept copyright Alec Finlay © 2008
Text copyright Alec Finlay © 2008
Drawings copyright Laurie Clark © 2008

Published in an edition of 750 copies

Designed by Alec Finlay and StudioLR
Printed and bound by Summerhall

With thanks to Alex Hodby and Linda France

ISBN 1-904477-06-2

www.alecfinlay.com
www.inglebygallery.com
www.jupiterartland.org